Highlights

LEARN-and-PLAY
Phonics
Spinner Games

For information about permission to reproduce selections from this book for an entire school or school district, please contact permissions@highlights.com.

Published by Highlights Learning
815 Church Street • Honesdale, Pennsylvania 1843¹
ISBN: 978-1-64472-833-8
Mfg. 08/2022
Printed in Shenzhen, Guangdong, China

First edition
10 9 8 7 6 5 4 3 2 1

For assistance in the preparation of this book, the editors would
Jump Start Press, Inc.; Vanessa Maldonado, MSEd; MS Literacy Ed. K–12;
Reading/LA Consultant Cert.; K–5 Literacy Instructional Coach

D1294903

Alphabet Adventure

HOW TO PLAY: Help the animals race through town from Ada's Art Shop to Zoe's Toy Shop. On each turn, spin and move to the next space of that color.

SPINNER KEY

● = red space   ● = yellow space   ● = blue space   ● = green space

Let's race!

Use the game pieces in the big envelope to mark where you land!

ADA'S ART SHOP

gift

H

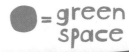
igloo

Start

F

J

A

E

DARCY'S DELI

keys

B

cat

duck

L

moo

If you land on a picture, say its name and the sound it starts with. If you land on a letter, trace it! Then name something that starts with that letter. Move your game piece from **Start** to **Finish** to win the game. If playing with 2 players, take turns!

You made it to Zoe's Toy Shop. Celebrate by singing and dancing to the alphabet song.

Can you say this tongue twister 3 times fast? Awesome animals are all around.

QUEENIE'S QUILTS

TOY SHOP

Finish

rainbow

seal

pumpkin

umbrella

yo-yo

wave

Trace and Race

HOW TO PLAY: Which monster will win the skate race to the playground? On each turn, spin for a color, and trace the next letter on that path. Then name something that starts with that letter sound.

The word monster starts with the m sound!

Ready, set, skate!

SPINNER KEY

● = red path   ● = yellow path   ● = blue path   ● = green path

It's a playground party!

m   M   m   M

Color the balloons the winning color!

t   T   t   T

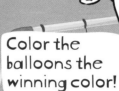

Give me a name that starts with M!

s   S   s   S

P   P   P   P

5

Search the Scenes

HOW TO PLAY: On each turn, spin for a color. Find a letter of that color in one of the scenes. Check it off! The first color with 5 checks wins.

Can you say this tongue twister 3 times fast? Time to trot to tasty treats!

Can you find at least **10** differences between the pictures?

SPINNER KEY

● = red **T** ☐ ☐ ☐ ☐ ☐

● = yellow t ☐ ☐ ☐ ☐ ☐

● = blue **T** ☐ ☐ ☐ ☐ ☐

● = green t ☐ ☐ ☐ ☐ ☐

Make a √ for each letter you find.

〓Draw an action card in the winning color!〓

Hidden Pictures Hunt

HOW TO PLAY: On each turn, find 1 hidden object that begins with the **s** sound. Then spin for a color. Use that color to fill in the object. After you find all 10 objects, the color used the most wins!

SPINNER KEY

 = red   = yellow   = blue   = green

≧ Draw an action card in the winning color! ≦

sandwich

sailboat

saw

seahorse

seal

seed

six

soap

sock

surfboard

Write the letter **s** to complete the word!

_____

un

Phonics Bingo

1 PLAYER: Can you get 4 in a row (across, down, or diagonally) in 8 spins or less?

2 PLAYERS: Player 1 uses the green board. Player 2 uses the purple board. The first player to circle 4 in a row wins!

mouse	pumpkin	tractor	sock
snowman	pig	mushroom	tree
moose	sweater	pie	tiger
plant	snail	mittens	turtle

HOW TO PLAY: On each turn, spin for a color and look at the spinner key below. Then circle something that starts with that letter sound.

SPINNER KEY

 = m   = t   = s   = p

sailboat	puppy	milk	teddy bear
mailbox	sun	truck	pear
monkey	slide	tire	pizza
table	pencil	map	seal

Color Contest

HOW TO PLAY: Help these puppies paint pumpkins! On each turn, spin for a color. Color in 1 pumpkin on the matching puppy's wagon. The first painter puppy with all 5 pumpkins colored in wins!

Can you say this tongue twister 3 times fast? Playful pups paint pumpkins.

What words do you know that start with p?

Rhyme Time Race

HOW TO PLAY: Help astronauts Abby and Ash get to Planet Amazing. On each turn, spin and move to the next space of that color.

SPINNER KEY

 = red space    = yellow space    = blue space   = green space

If you land on a picture, say the name of something that rhymes. If you land on a letter, trace it. Move your game piece from Start to Finish to win the game. If playing with 2 players, take turns!

> Use the game pieces to mark where you land!

Start

A

Pretend you are floating in space.

> Short a makes the ah sound, as in cat!

Spin like a planet.

a

bag

bat

A

nap

Take off at the speed of light. Move ahead 2 spaces.

Search the Scenes

HOW TO PLAY: On each turn, spin for a color. Find a letter of that color in one of the scenes. Check it off! The first color with 5 checks wins.

How do you go without a nap for nine days?

Nap at night!

Can you find at least **10** differences between the pictures?

SPINNER KEY

- ⬤ = red N
- ⬤ = yellow n
- ⬤ = blue N
- ⬤ = green n

[ ] [ ] [ ] [ ] [ ]
[ ] [ ] [ ] [ ] [ ]
[ ] [ ] [ ] [ ] [ ]
[ ] [ ] [ ] [ ] [ ]

Make a √ for each letter you find.

≥ Draw an action card in the winning color! ≤

Trace and Race

HOW TO PLAY: Which friend will win the football field race? On each turn, spin for a color, and trace the next letter on that path. Then name something that starts with that letter sound.

The word football starts with the **f** sound!

Just call me speedy!

SPINNER KEY

 = red path  = yellow path  = blue path  = green path

Color the goal post the winning color.

f F f F

d D d D

c C c C

b B b B

Make up a team name that starts with F!

19

Search the Scenes

HOW TO PLAY: On each turn, spin for a color. Find a letter of that color in one of the scenes. Check it off! The first color with 5 checks wins.

What do you call it when two dinosaurs crash into each other?

A Tyrannosaurus wreck!

Can you find at least **10** differences between the pictures?

SPINNER KEY

- ⬤ = red D
- ⬤ = yellow d
- ⬤ = blue D
- ⬤ = green d

Make a √ for each letter you find.

≥ Draw an action card in the winning color! ≤

Hidden Pictures Hunt

HOW TO PLAY: On each turn, find 1 hidden object that begins with the **b** sound. Then spin for a color. Use that color to fill in the object. After you find all 10 objects, the color used the most wins!

SPINNER KEY

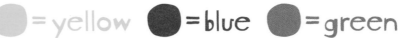 = red   = yellow   = blue   = green

≥ Draw an action card in the winning color! ≤

bandage   button   broom   backpack   banana

bucket   butterfly   bone   broccoli   belt

Write the letter **b** to complete the word!

_____
-----
unny
_____

Color Contest

HOW TO PLAY: On each turn, spin for a color. Color in 1 shape on the matching cow's car. The first cow with all 4 shapes colored in wins!

SPINNER KEY

● = red car ● = yellow car ● = blue car ● = green car

Draw an action card in the winning color!

Rhyme Time Race

HOW TO PLAY: Help Isabel and Ian ski to the igloo. On each turn, spin and move to the next space of that color.

SPINNER KEY

● = red space ● = yellow space ● = blue space ● = green space

If you land on a picture, say the name of something that rhymes. If you land on a letter, trace it. Move your game piece from **Start** to **Finish** to win the game. If playing with 2 players, take turns!

Use the game pieces to mark where you land!

| Start | I | Pretend to throw a snowball. |

Short i makes the ih sound, as in pig!

dig

| Say *BRR!* and shiver. | : |

zip

| I |  fin | You found a shortcut! Move ahead I space. |

Phonics Bingo

1 PLAYER: Can you get 4 in a row (across, down, or diagonally) in 8 spins or less?

2 PLAYERS: Player 1 uses the **green** board. Player 2 uses the **purple** board. The first player to circle 4 in a row wins!

cow	basket	rose	dart
rabbit	door	bow	coat
bee	carrot	dime	rhinoceros
doughnut	rain	car	button

SPINNER KEY

● =d ● =b ● =c ● =r

dinosaur	butterfly	candle	raccoon
cupcake	ring	dragonfly	bat
bird	cookie	rat	duck
rocket	bear	canoe	dog

Alphabet Adventure

HOW TO PLAY: Hank Hippo and Hilda Hippo are racing to the Happy Town roller coaster. On each turn, spin and move to the next space of that color.

SPINNER KEY

● = red space   ● = yellow space   ● = blue space   ● = green space

The word hippo starts with the h sound!

Start

Use the game pieces to mark where you land!

Spin like you are on the teacup ride.

house

banana

book

Pretend to drive a bumper car.

H

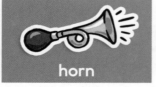
horn

horse

B

bird

cake

If you land on a picture, say its name and the sound it starts with. If you land on a letter, trace it! Then name something that starts with that letter. Move your game piece from **Start** to **Finish** to win the game. If playing with 2 players, take turns!

Cheer and raise your hands like you are on a wild ride!

Welcome to the Happy Town roller coaster!

C

caterpillar

rainbow

corn

robot

Stop for ice cream. Go back 1 space.

A crowd blocks your path! Go back 2 spaces

rabbit

Finish

R

Ride the trolley across the park. Move ahead 2 spaces.

31

Search the Scenes

HOW TO PLAY: On each turn, spin for a color. Find a letter of that color in one of the scenes. Check it off! The first color with 5 checks wins.

Can you say this tongue twister 3 times fast? Lea leaps on leaves!

Can you find at least **10** differences between the pictures?

SPINNER KEY

⬤ = red L

◯ = yellow l

⬤ = blue L

⬤ = green l

Make a √ for each letter you find.

≥ Draw an action card in the winning color! ≤

33

Color Contest

HOW TO PLAY: On each turn, spin for a color. Color in 1 music note next to the matching guitar. The first guitar player with all 4 music notes colored in wins!

The word goat starts with the hard-g sound.

The word giraffe starts with the soft-g sound.

Rhyme Time Race

HOW TO PLAY: Help Bob Dog and Todd Dog get to the hot-air balloon festival. On each turn, spin and move to the next space of that color.

SPINNER KEY

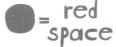 = red space  = yellow space  = blue space  = green space

If you land on a picture, say the name of something that rhymes. If you land on a letter, trace it. Move your game piece from **Start** to **Finish** to win the game. If playing with 2 players, take turns!

Use the game pieces to mark where you land!

Start

◯

Name something you might see from a hot-air balloon.

Short o makes the aw sound, as in dog!

fox

clock

Bark like a happy dog.

◯

◯

log

The wind pushes you forward. Move ahead 2 spaces!

Welcome to the hot-air balloon festival! Pretend to fly through the sky in a hot-air balloon.

Finish

 box

 dots

 frog

The wind pushes you back. Go back 1 space.

 Why don't balloons like school?

 sock

Birds fly in your way. Go back 2 spaces.

 They are afraid of pop quizzes.

 hop

 pot

You see a rainbow. Move ahead 1 space!

Trace and Race

HOW TO PLAY: Which kangaroo will win the race to King's Karate? On each turn, spin for a color, and trace the next letter on that path. Then name something that starts with that letter sound.

The word kangaroo starts with the k sound!

Jump, jump, kick!

SPINNER KEY

 = red path  = yellow path  = blue path  = green path

Can you say this tongue twister 3 times fast? Kevin Kangaroo can karate kick!

Color the flag the same color as the winning kangaroo's belt.

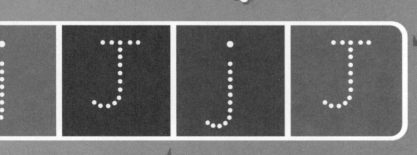

KING'S KARATE

Hidden Pictures Hunt

HOW TO PLAY: On each turn, find 1 hidden object that begins with the **w** sound. Then spin for a color. Use that color to fill in the object. After you find all 9 objects, the color used the most wins!

SPINNER KEY

 = red = yellow = blue = green

≋ Draw an action card in the winning color! ≋

whale

window

watermelon

whistle

wand

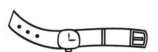

watch

work boot

worm

wishbone

Write the letter **w** to complete the word!

__et__

Alphabet Adventure

HOW TO PLAY: Jess Jellyfish and Jack Jellyfish are racing to the Jellyfish Diner. On each turn, spin and move to the next space of that color.

SPINNER KEY

 = red space   ○ = yellow space   ● = blue space   ○ = green space

The word jellyfish starts with the j sound!

Start

Make a silly fish face.

juice

Wiggle like a jellyfish's tentacles.

key

kite

Use the game pieces to mark where you land!

K

J

jacket

jet

koala

wate

If you land on a picture, say its name and the sound it starts with. If you land on a letter, trace it! Then name something that starts with that letter. Move your game piece from **Start** to **Finish** to win the game. If playing with 2 players, take turns!

Can you say this tongue twister 3 times fast? Jellyfish enjoy jam and juice!

You made it to the Jellyfish Diner! Rub your belly and say,"Yum!"

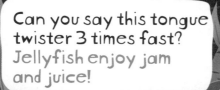

W

window

yak

Finish

watermelon

yogurt

Y

Stop and chat with a friend. Move back 2 spaces.

Catch a ride from a whale. Move ahead 2 spaces!

yo-yo

A wave carries you forward. Move ahead 1 space!

Phonics Bingo

1 PLAYER: Can you get 4 in a row (across, down, or diagonally) in 8 spins or less?

2 PLAYERS: Player 1 uses the green board. Player 2 uses the purple board. The first player to circle 4 in a row wins!

lamb	web	yarn	girl
gold	yoga	lock	walrus
whale	lemon	gorilla	yak
yam	glasses	worm	leaf

HOW TO PLAY: On each turn, spin for a color and look at the spinner key below. Then circle something that starts with that letter sound.

SPINNER KEY

● = l ● = g ● = w ● = y

yo-yo	wagon	golf club	lamp
ladybug	yellow	goat	wand
giraffe	world	ladder	yawn
lollipop	yolk	wheel	goose

Rhyme Time Race

HOW TO PLAY: Help Bucky Duck and Lucky Duck jump rope to Duck Park. On each turn, spin and move to the next space of that color.

SPINNER KEY

 = red space    = yellow space    = blue space    = green space

If you land on a picture, say the name of something that rhymes. If you land on a letter, trace it. Move your game piece from **Start** to **Finish** to win the game. If playing with 2 players, take turns!

Use the game pieces to mark where you land!

Start | U | Quack like a duck.

Short u makes the uh sound, as in duck!

 hug

Waddle like a duck. | U

 drum

U

 cub

You beat your jump rope record. Move ahead 2 spaces!

47

Color Contest

HOW TO PLAY: On each turn, spin for a color. Color in 1 square on the matching queen's quilt. The first queen with all 4 squares colored in wins!

Can you say this tongue twister 3 times fast? Queens quilt quickly.

Trace and Race

HOW TO PLAY: Which zebra will win the race to the zip line? On each turn, spin for a color, and trace the next letter on that path. Then name something that starts with that letter sound.

The word zebra starts with the z sound!

This zebra is ready to zip-line!

Z Z Z Z

V V V V

X X X X

e E e E

Can you say this tongue twister 3 times fast? Zany zebras zig, zag, zip!

Color my shirt the winning color!

Hidden Pictures Hunt

HOW TO PLAY: On each turn, find 1 hidden object that begins with the **v** sound. Then spin for a color. Use that color to fill in the object. After you find all 10 objects, the color used the most wins!

SPINNER KEY

 = red = yellow = blue = green

≷ Draw an action card in the winning color! ≷

vest

valentine

vacuum

vase

viper

vine

violin

volcano

volleyball

vegetable

Write the letter **v** to complete the word!

 et

Search the Scenes

HOW TO PLAY: On each turn, spin for a color. Find a letter of that color in one of the scenes. Check it off! The first color with 5 checks wins.

Can you say this tongue twister 3 times fast? Max Fox has a box!

Can you find at least 10 differences between the pictures?

SPINNER KEY

- 🔴 = red X
- 🟡 = yellow x
- 🔵 = blue X
- 🟢 = green x

☰Draw an action card in the winning color!☰

Make a √ for each letter you find.

Rhyme Time Race

HOW TO PLAY: Help Deb Jet and Glen Jet fly to the airport! On each turn, spin and move to the next space of that color.

SPINNER KEY

 = red space    = yellow space    = blue space    = green space

If you land on a picture, say the name of something that rhymes. If you land on a letter, trace it. Move your game piece from **Start** to **Finish** to win the game. If playing with 2 players, take turns!

Use the game pieces to mark where you land!

Start   E   Roar like a jet engine!

Short e makes the eh sound, as in jet!

 bed

 vest   Spin like a daring jet.   e

E    dress   The wind gives you a lift. Move ahead 2 spaces!

Welcome to the airport! Stretch your arms and pretend to fly like a jet.

Finish

pen

shed

E

pet

The ride is bumpy. Go back 1 space.

e

What do you call an elephant that flies?

nest

e

Dark clouds block your path. Go back 2 spaces.

net

A jumbo jet!

e

hen

The sky is clear today. Move ahead 1 space!

E

Hidden Pictures Hunt

HOW TO PLAY: On each turn, find 1 short-vowel object. Then spin for a color. Use that color to fill in the object. After you find all 10 objects, the color used the most wins!

SPINNER KEY

⬤ = red ⬤ = yellow ⬤ = blue ⬤ = green

nut	fan	net	jet	bib

twig	mop	frog	mug	can

Where do books sleep?

Under their covers

Phonics Bingo

1 PLAYER: Can you get 4 in a row (across, down, or diagonally) in 8 spins or less?

2 PLAYERS: Player 1 uses the green board. Player 2 uses the purple board. The first player to circle 4 in a row wins!

crab	fin	dog	cup
pig	plant	sock	duck
mom	red	bag	six
sled	bot	kid	hat

HOW TO PLAY: On each turn, spin for a color and look at the spinner key below. Then circle something that has that short-vowel sound.

SPINNER KEY

 = a ● = e ● = i ● = o or u

chick	clock	tent	bat
flag	slug	fish	log
truck	pin	fox	lamp
shell	twins	rocks	cab

Alphabet Adventure

HOW TO PLAY: Fox and Crab are racing to the outer space Grand Slam. On each turn, spin and move to the next space of that color.

SPINNER KEY

● = red space   ● = yellow space   ● = blue space   ● = green space

Use the game pieces to mark where you land!

Start

Can you say this tongue twister 3 times fast? Crab's cab can catch up to Fox's box.

Pretend to swing a baseball bat.

den

Make a wish on a shooting star.

wet

big

can

mad

tip

jo

If you land on a word, read the word, and say its vowel sound. If you land on a letter, trace it! Then name something that has that short-vowel sound. Move your game piece from Start to Finish to win the game. If playing with 2 players, take turns!

You made it to the Grand Slam! Celebrate by cheering for your favorite team.

CIDER

TICKETS

fun

Buy tickets for the game. Move ahead 2 spaces!

Finish

not

O

cut

U

Your ship gets a rocket boost. Move ahead I space!

You got space dust in your eye. Go back I space.

You make a wrong turn. Go back I space.

Answers

Pages 6-7
Search the Scenes

Page 9
Hidden Pictures Hunt

Pages 16-17
Search the Scenes

You did great!

Pages 20-21
Search the Scenes

Page 23
Hidden Pictures Hunt